LIBERATION THEOLOGY

The Paradigm Shift

M.D. LITONJUA

University Press of America, Inc.
Lanham • New York • Oxford

Copyright © 1998 by
University Press of America,® Inc.
4720 Boston Way
Lanham, Maryland 20706

12 Hid's Copse Rd.
Cummor Hill, Oxford OX2 9JJ

Library of Congress Cataloging-in-Publication Data

Litonjua, M. D.
Liberation theology : the paradigm shift / M.D. Litonjua.
p.   cm.
Includes bibliographical references and index.
l. Liberation theology. I. Title.
BT83.57.L5   1997   230'.0464--dc21   97--39632 CIP

ISBN 0-7618-0928-7 (cloth: alk. ppr.)
ISBN 0-7618-0929-5 (pbk: alk. ppr.)

⊖™ The paper used in this publication meets the minimum
requirements of American National Standard for information
Sciences—Permanence of Paper for Printed Library Materials,
ANSI Z39.48—1984

Contents

Preface

I was first of all a student of theology before I became a student of sociology. After my formal studies in theology and while I was involved in the deepening problems of Philippine society in the 1970s, I got acquainted with Latin American liberation theology. It immediately resonated with what I was trying to do, opening up areas in the life of faith hitherto closed, making sense of the relationship of the twofold commandment of love to actual socio-political realities, giving direction to commitments grounded in hope.

But there was much that I could not understand about liberation theology: social structures, institutionalized violence, structural injustice, social sin. I started studying sociology. The basic approach of sociology is to consider religion one of the five basic social institutions of society. Religion is a group phenomenon that is subject to the social processes which all social reality undergoes. I discovered that there was much that sociology could contribute to theology. Sociology can clarify and illuminate from a different perspective much that is happening in religion and the Church.

This monograph is an example of such a fruitful and enlightening crossbreeding. I utilize Thomas Kuhn's sociological theory of scientific revolutions, and contend that a momentous shift in theological paradigms is involved in liberation theology. I elaborate on this by developing the cognitive nature of the liberation paradigm and its community structure. By advancing a sociological understanding of theological knowledge, theological knowledge itself is enhanced, its social and ecclesial contexts better appreciated, its development and directions more clearly delineated.

Introduction

ഔരൂ

There is a variety of liberation theologies today, which ranges from black and feminist liberation theologies in the United States to emerging liberation theologies in Asia and Africa, all sharing the fundamental concern with liberation from oppression, but differing in their emphases due to different forms of oppression. But the prototype of liberation theology is Latin American liberation theology. It was the first to emerge,[1] and has become the most developed in terms of the growing body of literature specifically devoted to it and of the expanding theological areas in which its concerns have been applied. Most importantly, it provided an exemplar in a new method of doing theology, and established therefore a new model of theologizing followed by subsequent liberation theologies.

Gutierrez (1973: 6), the dean of Latin American liberation theologians, defined the theology of liberation as "critical reflection on praxis," and originally understood it as an added function to the classical theological tasks of rational knowledge and spiritual wisdom, but one which rescues them from the division and deformations they have suffered throughout history. "The critical function of theology necessarily leads to redefinition of these other two tasks. Henceforth wisdom and rational knowledge will more explicitly have ecclesial praxis as their point of departure and their context. It is in reference to this praxis that an understanding of spiritual growth based on Scripture should be developed, and it is through this same praxis that faith encounters the problems posed by human reason" (Gutierrez 1973: 13-14).

Later authors, developments, and literature make the point that Latin American liberation theology involves and demands a different hermeneutic on doing theology that affects all theology. "The phrase 'theology of liberation' does not designate one sector of theology (such as the 'theology of work' or the 'theology of death')," Segundo (1974: 105) is emphatic, "but the whole of theology itself." In this sense, Gremillion (1976: 136) believes that Latin American liberation theology is "the first school of theological thought to arise outside Western Europe since that of the Cappadocians and Eastern Church colleagues of 400-600 A.D."

In this monograph, I propose to provide an understanding of Latin American liberation theology by utilizing the theory of paradigm change that Kuhn (1970) developed to explain scientific revolutions. First, I will outline the salient features of Kuhn's structure of scientific revolutions that are analogously applicable in understanding the changes involved in liberation theology. Then I will indicate the social and ecclesial contexts — the broader historical and social realities neglected by Kuhn — in which Latin American liberation theology emerged and which gave rise to it. Lastly, I will discuss the cognitive nature of the paradigm of liberation theology — what exactly constitutes the new paradigm of liberation theology? — and the community structure of its practitioners — what made it possible to emerge in Latin America and how was the paradigm shift maintained? The article proposes to advance a sociological understanding of theological knowledge. The Kuhnian theory of scientific revolutions clarifies the fundamental shift involved in Latin American liberation theology.

Chapter I

ℬⓈⓇ

The Kuhnian Theory of Paradigm Change

Kuhn's *The Structure of Scientific Revolutions* has become the most influential and debated book in the history, philosophy, and sociology of science since it was published in 1962. Its impact has been felt in diverse fields of inquiry, leading students of various disciplines to assess the utility and relevance of his theory of scientific revolutions to their own concerns (Gutting 1980). An international symposium was even convoked to discuss the relevance and applicability of paradigm change to the entire history and field of theology (Kung and Tracy 1989; see also Barbour 1990). Kung (1992, 1995) has applied the theory of paradigm change in his surveys of the historical development of the world's monotheistic religions, two of which have been published on Judaism and Christianity, and the third of which is forthcoming on Islam. In fact, Kuhn (1970: 136) discussed "one of the aspects of scientific work that most clearly distinguishes it from every other creative pursuit except perhaps theology," i.e., the writing of textbooks that hides the abrupt turns and shifts involved in paradigm changes. Thus, while Kuhn's original explication of the structure of scientific revolutions was drawn from the natural sciences, it has been utilized and applied analogously to developments in other disciplines.

In contrast to the prevailing image of scientific change and development as a linear process of cumulative knowledge, Kuhn argued that scientific revolutions which are non-cumulative developmental episodes play a greater role in scientific development, and they occur when an older paradigm is replaced in whole or in part by a new paradigm. Thus, the discrete quantum leaps in scientific advancement from Ptolemy to Copernicus in astronomy, from Priestley to Lavoisier in chemistry, and from Newton to Einstein in physics were not mere accretions to accumulated bodies of knowledge, but each constituted "a transformation of the scientific imagination" which resulted in a new conceptual framework through which scientists viewed reality and the world. The new way of seeing was made possible by a change in paradigms.

Kuhn's original formulation was quite vague and confusing. Paradigms were "universally recognized scientific achievements that for a time provide model problems and solutions to a community of practitioners" (Kuhn 1970: viii). Masterman (1970) contended that there are at least twenty-one different ways in which the term is used in Kuhn's book, and reduced Kuhn's various uses to three categories: metaphysical, sociological, and construct paradigms. At the broadest level of generality, paradigm refers to unquestioned presuppositions, meta-theoretical assumptions regarding the object of study, which are not usually made explicit, but which underlie and guide research and study. More restricted is the meaning of paradigm as a disciplinary matrix which represents the shared commitments of a disciplinary community, including symbolic generalizations, beliefs, and values. And the most restricted use is paradigms as exemplars, referring to the concrete accomplishments of a scientific community which serve as shared examples, "a time-tested and group-licensed way of seeing," (Kuhn 1970: 189) in concrete problem-solving.

In a postscript to the second edition of his book, Kuhn (1970: 187) states that "the paradigm as shared example is the central element of what I take to be the most novel and least understood aspect of this book." Paradigms as concrete examples of scholarship that serve as models for further research and study constitute the most central and deepest meaning of paradigms for Kuhn. Masterman (1970: 77; Eckberg and Hill 1980: 119) further helps to pin down the significance of paradigms by pointing out that the most important question is not what an exemplar *is* so much as what it *does*.

Two aspects are central to the theory of paradigm change: the cognitive nature of the paradigm, and the community structure of its practitioners. A paradigm provides the framework of assumptions, disciplinary matrix, and exemplars with which a community of scholars pursues its work. It defines the types of questions that may legitimately be asked, the types of explanations that must be sought, the types of solutions that are considered acceptable, as well as, the methods of inquiry suitable for studying them.

But what is equally, if not more, important is the structure of the group which collectively holds a paradigm. A community of scientists provides the possibility for a consensus with regard to assumptions, symbolic generalizations, beliefs, values and, most of all, exemplars which constitute a paradigm. A shared paradigm creates a scientific community: a professional grouping with common assumptions, interests, journals, and channels of communication. Thus, a paradigm both presupposes and demands an integrated community of practitioners. The communal nature of a paradigm is of the essence of the concept, and constitutes the sociological base of Kuhn's theory of scientific revolutions. In fact, Kuhn (1970: 176) in his aforementioned postscript writes that "if this book were being rewritten, it would therefore open with a discussion of the community structure of science."

The period of "normal science" is characterized by the stability of a paradigm. Normal scientific activity primarily consists in "puzzle-solving" within the confines of the dominant paradigm. The members of the scientific community undertake their work, pursue their efforts within the boundaries of the accepted paradigm; they do not question but accept, explicitly or implicitly, the assumptions, the disciplinary matrix, and the exemplars of the given paradigm. They are locked in, as it were, within the worldview of the established framework which guides the direction of normal research. Anomalies are set to one side, or accommodated by *ad hoc* modifications. Normal scientific activity is essentially one of building on previous research based on the accepted paradigm, of finding answers to still outstanding questions with the use and within the purview of the same paradigm. This is the image of scientific knowledge as standing "on the shoulders of giants" (Merton 1985).

When problems accumulate and "puzzles" mount that remain impervious to solution despite repeated attempts to solve them within the framework of the given paradigm, the state of "normal science" gives way to a period of crisis. Crisis leads the scientific community to examine its assumptions and to search for alternatives. Doubts and questions are raised about the paradigm itself, about its symbols, beliefs, values, and exemplars. The period of crisis is a period in which questions of basic theoretical and methodological significance are examined. The hitherto coherent scientific tradition with its networks of conceptual, theoretical, instrumental, and methodological commitments is subjected to ferment and turmoil. Out of the crisis, a new paradigm emerges — or several new ones or parts of new ones appear — which challenges the worldview of the old dominant paradigm.

When the new paradigm shows itself supreme over the old paradigm in its capacity to solve problems and puzzles left unsolved, it gains ascendancy and acceptance, initially by a small group of practitioners. When the new paradigm earns general acceptance by the scientific community at large, the old paradigm is displaced and declared bankrupt, and the new paradigm becomes the dominant exemplar in scientific research. Scientific activity returns once more to the state of normal science. In this way were achieved the enormous advances from geocentric to heliocentric theory in astronomy, from phlogiston to oxygen theory in chemistry, and from corpuscular to wave theory in physics.

A major change of paradigms has far-reaching consequences that it amounts to a scientific revolution.

Scientists usually resist such upheavals which subvert assumptions and commitments that have permeated their thinking. Adoption of a new paradigm demands a gestalt switch which produces a consequent shift in views, a new way of raising questions and seeking solutions worthy of scientific inquiry. It involves a veritable "conversion" of the scientific imagination which results in the transformation not only of the world in which scientific work is pursued but also of the world which is the very object of scientific work.

From this it becomes apparent that Kuhn has moved beyond the traditional concerns of the sociology of science. Weingart (1974; also King 1980) has written that Kuhn has not only attained the stature of Merton in the sociology of science, but has replaced him in the basic constellation of problems that the sociology of science has to tackle. Merton (1973) made a sharp distinction between science as a cognitive system and science as a social system, and as a sociologist proffered competency only over the latter. Kuhn's ideas, on the other hand, both apply to the content and methodology of science and account for the sociological underpinning of scientific ideas and methods. To formulate it differently: unlike Merton's approach, Kuhn does not separate the cognitive system and the social system of science. Paradigm stability and change, normal science and scientific revolutions involve both the cognitive and social systems of science. Changes in the cognitive and social systems of science account for paradigm change and scientific revolutions.

Chapter II

ഇറ

The Broader Social and Ecclesial Contexts

The formulation of liberation theology, so radical in its implications for Latin America where the vast majority of the population is baptized Catholics, who, at the same time, are immersed in grinding poverty, cannot be understood fully without considering the changes in the wider social and ecclesial realities that laid down the necessary conditions to make its emergence possible. The impact of such broader historical and social forces is what is lacking in Kuhn's structure of scientific revolutions, since he attends only to the internal structures of the scientific enterprise. It is a necessary corrective to Kuhn's theory of paradigm change to broaden the sociological inquiry into these factors that make for paradigm crisis and paradigm change. No intellectual current is born in a social and historical vacuum; historical and social realities

provide the necessary contexts to study the emergence
and development of paradigmatic ideas.

Dependency and Underdevelopment

The broader historical and social context that provided
the conditions for the possibility of Latin American
liberation theology has to be situated in the decolonization
process in the 1950s when one country after another in
Africa gained its independence. Together with the long-
independent countries of Latin America and the equally-
recently independent nations of Asia, they formed the
poor, underdeveloped countries of the Third World and
became the object of study, research, and efforts to bring
them into the modern world. The United Nations declared
the 1960s the Decade of Development, and President
Kennedy launched the Alliance for Progress, intended to
bring about the development of the Third World and of
Latin America respectively.

These development efforts were conceptually
undergirded by modernization theory which posited as
goal and model the modern Western nation, and assumed
that Third World countries could simply follow the path
trodden by developed and industrialized countries. The
immediate social context for the rise of Latin American
liberation theology was the failure of development
programs — since then pejoratively referred to as
developmentalism, *desarollismo* — to solve underdevelopment and to achieve social transformation. In fact,
many development efforts resulted in substantial upward
redistribution: the rich grew richer, the middle class got
nothing, and the poor were worse off. The promise of
economic growth did not trickle down to the masses.

An alternative theoretical framework in analyzing the historically distinctive problems of the Third World soon came to be utilized, the dependency approach to underdevelopment. For *dependencistas*, the basic context of poverty and underdevelopment is the dominance-dependence relationship between rich and poor, powerful and weak countries. The development of the rich countries brought about and continues to maintain the underdevelopment of the poor countries. Instead of modernization theory's continuum from traditional to modern, therefore, underdevelopment is the counterpart of development. Countries of the Third World are not merely undeveloped, but are *under*developed.

Dependency looked back at colonization which Third World countries share in their histories as the starting point of its analysis. The centuries of colonialism pillaged these countries of their natural resources, left them economies oriented to meet the demands of the outside world, instead of the basic necessities of their populations, erected social institutions that structured inequalities in the social order. Even with political independence, economic relationships with dominant economies continue to be unbalanced and unjust, rendering Third World countries vulnerable to and at the mercy of the vagaries of the world economy.

The dominance-dependence relationship, moreover, is internalized within the Third World country. This is the fact of internal colonialism. Tiny minorities of elites in underdeveloped countries, whose origins lie in colonial history, control the economic and political systems of their countries, collude with the transnational interests of developed countries, act as bridgeheads in the maintenance of the subservient status of their peoples, and reap the benefits of whatever economic growth there is.

The result is that the gap between rich and poor sectors within the poor country is added to the gap between rich and poor countries. The spiral of growth is moving upward and is becoming smaller and richer. The spiral of immiseration is falling downward and is growing larger and poorer.

There has been much controversy about dependency (Packenham 1992). The original formulation by Frank (1969a, 1969b) has been rejected as too simplistic, especially his contention that dependency always equals stagnation. The historical, structural, and dialectical approach of Cardoso (Cardoso and Faletto 1979) in the analysis of concrete situations of dependency is considered more useful and fruitful. Such an approach, for one, allows for the possibility of associated-dependent development (Cardoso 1973) which in the case of Brazil was brought about by the triple alliance of local, state, and multinational capital (Evans 1979).

Most controversial was the prescription of some *dependencistas* that the way out of dependency and into self-sufficiency lies in revolution and socialism. With the collapse of the Soviet Union and the "velvet revolution" in Eastern Europe, that option has become less tenable, if at all. The abysmal failure of authoritarian regimes in Latin America in improving the lot of their populations has brought about a new appreciation of formal democracy and the space it affords in promoting social change and development.

The significance of dependency lies in the fact that it constituted an epistemological break in development theory, a break in which the stark contrasts drawn by Frank played a not insignificant role (Foster-Carter 1976). In particular, dependency has two distinctive features that make its contributions of continuing relevance. First, it is a perspective primarily generated by scholars in the Third World. Dependency is a view from the underside of history, from below the international structures of power, from the point of the poor peoples of the world as they experience the domination of powerful nations and their subordination to the latter's interests. Second, dependency is less of a formal theory than "a methodology for the analysis of concrete situations of under-development" (Evans 1993: 232). For those who use dependency and find it meaningful, development is his-torically open-ended and its directions of change cannot be fully predicted. Dependency continues to be an important point of departure and a methodological guide in the comparative study of poverty and under-development.

Vatican II and Medellin

The Second Vatican Ecumenical Council, convoked by Pope John XXIII in 1962 to bring about an *aggiornamento* in the Catholic Church, was the landmark ecclesial event that made possible the theological thinking that led to Latin American liberation theology. This is true for practically all subsequent efforts at renewal and reform in the Catholic Church. Vatican II effectively called into question important presuppositions and conceptualizations of the hitherto dominant theological paradigm. John XXIII's *aggiornamento* had the effect of legitimizing the criticisms of, and challenges to, traditional theological thought that had resulted from developments in biblical, historical, and liturgical research; it articulated the problems posed by the continued use of intellectual categories no longer compatible with modern thinking, the difficulties encountered in preaching the Christian message, couched in traditional terminology, to contemporary men and women. The renewal and reforms of Vatican II wrought changes in the self-understanding of the Church and its relationship to other churches and religions; they brought about a new appreciation of the human world and human history in all their diversity and dimensions. The net result was to undermine the foundations of the hitherto supreme Tridentine theological paradigm, and to open up the tight and narrow confines within which the theological task could be pursued.

Two documents of the Council were especially significant: the Constitution on the Church, *Lumen Gentium*, and the Pastoral Constitution on the Church in the Modern World, *Gaudium et Spes* (Abbott 1966). *Lumen Gentium* contained the idea of the Church as the People of God, a community characterized by a fundamental equality and a common responsibility. Before the hierarchy of office, power, and privilege between episcopate, clergy, and laity, there is first of all their fundamental unity, equality, and solidarity as the People of God, and their common responsibility as a sign and instrument of God's kingdom. *Gaudium et Spes* contained the principle of the Church as servant, a community in service to humanity and the world. The Church partakes of the joys and hopes, the griefs and anxieties of all humanity, especially of those who are poor. These two documents accomplished a redefinition of the self-identity of the Church and its mission to the world. The Church is the People of God on pilgrimage on this earth in which it has the responsibility to work for justice, peace, and love. In fact, during the Council, a vocal minority of Third World bishops lobbied for a "Church of the Poor," issuing a declaration in 1966 which went far beyond the Council documents in committing the Church to the poor of the Third World; their leader was Dom Helder Camara from the impoverished northeast of Brazil.

But even before the Council ended, Pope John had issued his encyclicals, *Mater et Magistra* (1961) and *Pacem in Terris* (1963), which broadened Church concerns to issues of poverty, education, and political participation, and of justice, war, and peace in a nuclear age. *Pacem in Terris* was the first papal encyclical addressed to "all men of good will" which, in turn, evoked an unprecedented favorable response from all quarters. After the Council, Pope Paul VI issued his encyclical, *Populorum Progressio* (1967), by far the most progressive of all social encyclicals till then, in which he called attention to the scandalous poverty and underdevelopment of Third World peoples, and condemned the international imperialism of money as the chief obstacle to the integral human development of peoples.

In August-September of 1968, the Second Conference of the Latin American Episcopate (CELAM) convened at Medellin, Colombia, to respond to Vatican II and *Populorum Progressio*, to apply their teachings to the specific conditions of Latin America, a continent mired in massive poverty and misery. Medellin, where the Latin American Church consciously expressed its own identity, is for liberation theology what Vatican II is for the universal Church in importance and meaning. It was a turning point for the Latin American Church, and it provided the immediate ecclesial context for the emergence of a new theological paradigm.

Medellin carried out an epistemological break from the mainstream concerns of the dominant Western theological tradition, especially of European liberal theology. Confronted by the massive misery of their continent and questioning the role of the Church which from colonial days had been in alliance with wealth and power, the bishops at Medellin continued the theological shift effected at Vatican II and followed it along new pathways. Addressing themselves to the socio-political dimensions of the Christian faith and committing themselves to the liberation of their peoples from oppression, they brought about a change in theological outlook and direction, an alteration in theological assumptions and concerns, a shift in theological method and content. Medellin's changed outlook, direction, and project were shared by a community of theologians which constituted the sociological base for the emergence and maintenance of the new paradigm of liberation theology.

One key idea in the documents of CELAM (1970) at Medellin was that of structural injustice and institutionalized violence. The problems of Latin America did not lie with the personal deficiencies of its peoples, but were built into the social structures which since the colonial past had benefitted the few at the expense of the many. These social structures of inequality and injustice marginalize, oppress, and exploit the poor, and perpetrate institutionalized violence on them. The counterparts to structural injustice and institutionalized violence are liberation and participation. Liberation was, and is, understood in the biblical sense of physical and spiritual salvation from oppression and sin, historically typified in the Exodus of the Hebrew Scriptures and announced as Good News by Christ. But a people cannot be free unless they understand what keeps them from being free and what emancipation and freedom mean and entail. Thus, the Medellin documents place priority on a "liberating education," through which the poor become critically conscious of the structures of unfreedom and domination, and on grassroots Christian communities (*comunidades de base*), through which people's participation and self-reliance can be encouraged and achieved. Medellin produced the Magna Carta of the socially committed Latin American Church, shattering its centuries-old alliance with the propertied and the powerful in a continent of poverty and oppression. That thrust, however, had to struggle to be vindicated at Puebla in 1979 (Eagleson and Scharper 1979), and it barely survived at Santo Domingo in 1992 (Hennelly 1993).

The conjunction of the rethinking on under-development by dependency and the reforms of Vatican II and Medellin provided the broader historical, social, and ecclesial contexts for the paradigm crisis and change that gave rise to Latin American liberation theology. For McGovern (1989a: 273), dependency theory "played an instrumental role in the very articulation of a theology of liberation. The new theology rejected 'developmental' policies and called explicitly for 'liberation' from dependency." The epistemological break and methodology accomplished by dependency in development studies were carried out in the epistemological break and methodology effected by liberation theology in theological studies. The new paradigm of dependency in development studies gave rise to the new paradigm of liberation in theology.

Chapter III

ℬℭℜ

The Cognitive Nature of the Liberation Paradigm

Ever since the Council of Trent (1545-1564) which culminated the Catholic reaction to the Protestant Reformation, a dominant theological paradigm, enforced by the authority of Rome, guided theological reflection and study. The worldwide community of Catholic theologians pursued their theological task within the framework and worldview of the underlying assumptions and values, the disciplinary matrix, and exemplars of the dominant Tridentine paradigm.

In the ensuing years, liturgical, scriptural, historical, and theological studies raised questions and problems about the Tridentine theological paradigm. At the time of the Second Vatican Council, the dominant paradigm was in crisis, as a result of which Vatican II initiated a break and a shift to a new theological focus and method.

Medellin and liberation theology continued the shift by specifying further a new focus and methodology.

What is cognitively new about the liberation paradigm is not so much its content as its method. To put it better: because of a different focus and method of doing theology, liberation theology uncovers new insights, pursues new lines of inquiry, and reaches new conclusions regarding the content of theology. What is new in the theological content and conclusions of liberation theology is arrived at via a different methodology which constitutes the essence of the liberation paradigm. The paradigm shift that liberation theology accomplished can best be understood by discussing three aspects of the cognitive nature, specifically of the methodological approach, of the liberation paradigm: theology as critical reflection on praxis, theology addressed to non-persons, and theology of and *for* liberation.

Theology as Critical Reflection on Praxis

Tridentine theology started with God and his revelation, primarily understood objectively as the truths revealed by God for human salvation. The focus was on the content of revelation — the deposit of faith — its explanation and defense against attacks, its systematization and the elaboration of its implications. The central traditional concern was *intellectus fidei*, the understanding of the mysteries of the Catholic faith, which decided the value of practice, the morality of action, the merit of life. The human person's stance was one of acceptance and conformity: acceptance of God's revelation as authoritatively taught by the Church, and conformity to what it demands and implies for the Christian life. The theological task primarily, if not exclusively, attended to faith as a gift from God mediated through biblical symbols, doctrine, sacraments, and Church institution. Orthodoxy was required: soundness in religious doctrine, fidelity to the correct understanding of faith in teaching and preaching.

Vatican II attended, first of all, to revelation as God revealing himself and his love. In *Gaudium et Spes*, it enjoins Christians to discern the signs of the times in the aspirations of contemporary men and women, in the events and happenings in the world, and to respond to them in faith and love. Revelation is ongoing. God continues to reveal himself and his love, and he continues to call people to respond to him in love. This shift in understanding of revelation and faith results in a different way of doing theology.

Theology has to start with the human person and human experiences, with the world and the human condition. Anthropology is its original meaning as the study of the human person, not narrowly as the study of the origins of the human species, becomes a necessary and preliminary dimension of the theological task. Thus, to mention but one example, Tracy (1975: 32) has proposed "what seems clearly to be the central task of contemporary Christian theology: the dramatic confrontation, the mutual illuminations and corrections, the possible basic reconciliation between the principal values, cognitive claims, and existential faiths of both a reinterpreted postmodern consciousness and a reinterpreted Christianity."

Latin American liberation theology further extends this epistemological shift in the theological task by

attending not just to any human experience and human
condition, but specifically to the human experience of
misery and oppression, to the human condition of poverty
and underdevelopment which characterize Latin American
nations and peoples. It situates theological reflection and
study within the context of the need to emancipate from
oppression, of the duty to liberate from the social
structures of injustice and sin. Liberation theology
demands, therefore, a prior commitment to, and involvement in, the liberation struggle; it is the fruit of
participation in the actual practice of liberation. "Before
we can do theology," the Boffs (1987: 22) put it, "we
have to 'do' liberation." Liberation theology arises out
of a concrete social situation in need of liberation; it is
the reflection on the efforts to bring about and achieve
liberation. Thus, Gutierrez (1973: 13) defines liberation
theology as "a critical reflection on Christian praxis in
the light of the Word."

Social practice and social analysis, therefore, precede
theological reflection. Like Hegel's famous owl of
Minerva that appears only at dusk, Gutierrez (1973: 11)
underscores that "theology *follows*; it is the second step."
Theology proper comes in only as a second moment after
the required preliminary steps have been undertaken: that
of experiencing, understanding, and analyzing the social
situation in need of liberation; that of committing oneself
to the task and the goal of liberation, of participating in,
and suffering from, liberation efforts and struggles. In a
different but clarifying vein, Steeman (1973: 45) explains:

> It is not the Church [nor theology, for that matter]
> which determines what the problems of the world are;
> it is the world in its factuality which presents itself to
> the Christian community as a problem. In more

technical terms we can say that non-theological data becomes decisive in shaping the mind of the Christian community. This means that the Christian community in its political involvement defines itself as open to the world and as willing to shape itself in such a way as to be able to serve the world.

But the second moment of theological reflection is not merely juxtaposing social practice with, and correlating it to, biblical symbols and Christian meanings, especially as the latter have been traditionally understood and expressed. The theological task for liberation theology demands *orthopraxis*, the dialectical unity of action and reflection: the oppressive reality and liberating practice confront and challenge the traditional understanding of the Christian message, the perennial symbols of the Christian faith; renewed theological understanding and revitalized Christian symbols, in turn, further illumine and inspire the hope of the liberation struggle. Theological reflection is not an autonomous but a dialectical process: it involves questioning and re-interpreting the revealed mysteries of the Christian faith as it attempts to respond to and answer the questions and problems posed by unjust social structures and sin and the efforts to transform them. Theological science, paraphrasing Cone (1970: 1), is the study of God's revelation not in itself, but as it confronts the existential situation of an oppressed community, relating the struggle for liberation with the Gospel of Jesus Christ; it is the ordered meaning of God's Word in the world which recognizes and shows that the inner thrust for liberation is not only consistent with but is of the essence of the Christian message.

The two fundamental moments of liberation theology are of the greatest epistemological and methodological import and indicate most clearly the change in theological paradigm. In the framework of liberation theology, Gutierrez (1994: 549) asserts that "the distinction of two phases (the first act and second act) is a key element in theological method." Let me recapitulate by indicating some problematic areas. The first moment is constituted by an option for the poor and social analysis. First, there is the fundamental option in faith for liberation, a basic value that orients the analysis of the social situation and the consequent theological reflection on it. This prior option leads to the rejection of value-freedom which is posited as the ideal of scientific inquiry, but which in practice results in the non-recognition of metatheoretical factors. (We shall elaborate on the preferential option for the poor in the next section.) Then follows the analysis of the social situation, especially as experienced and acted upon by efforts to change it.

Latin American liberation theologians, especially at the beginning, accepted and utilized the analysis of underdevelopment of Latin America provided by the socio-economic theory which focused on the socio-political concept of dependency. It was this use of social analysis that ignited often vehement attacks against liberation theology as "Marxist." But as McGovern (1989a, 1989b), in the most comprehensive assessment of liberation theology and its critics, has shown, the charge of Marxism is overblown and misplaced. Besides, conventional economic analysis of Third World countries (e.g. Todaro 1989) does not exactly invalidate the main tenets of dependency analysis. At any rate, the importance once given to Marxist concepts and dependency issues in liberation theology has since diminished, and their limitations accepted. Gutierrez (1988), on the occasion of the fifteenth anniversary of his classic text, has even changed the title of one section from "Christian Brotherhood and Class Struggle" to "Faith and Social Conflict" to avoid misunderstandings. However, the preliminary need for and the critical use of the social sciences remain, as Gutierrez (1990) elaborated in a long essay, in the study of social reality for the purposes of better understanding its problems, challenges, and possibilities. Just as scholastic theology needed Aristotelian philosophical concepts to explicate theological mysteries and truths, just as insights on personality development and psychological maturity throw a light on moral and spiritual growth, just as a better understanding of biological and human processes helps clarify the morality of human actions, so the social sciences serve as the handmaiden to liberation theology.

The non-theological data of social analysis provide the raw materials for theological reflection in the second moment. This is not to say that the world sets the agenda for the Church, that social science determines the perspective of Christianity or the horizons of faith. Nor does theological reflection simply mean the juxtaposed application or the uncritical correlation of past biblical symbols and traditional Christian meanings to the present. The process is dialectical. The world in its crises summons the Church and theology in each particular generation to decipher the signs of the times and to respond to them by incarnating themselves anew, assuming what has not yet been redeemed. Theological reflection leading to new forms of faith seriously takes into account the structures of the present which limit the range of human options and set the priorities for Christian action. The Christian past is certainly the norm that criticizes and judges the present, but equally the historical present must criticize and judge the norm, the understanding of which was achieved in a given historical period and since then absolutized for all times. The biblical past and the historical present stand as full dialogical partners for the sake of the eschatological future.

Segundo (1976: 9) presents his liberative methodology differently, by utilizing the concept of "the hermeneutic circle," in which four steps are delineated. It has implications for the tasks both of social analysis in the first moment and of theological reflection in the second moment.

> *Firstly* there is our way of experiencing reality, which leads us to ideological suspicion. *Secondly* there is the application of our ideological suspicion to the whole ideological superstructure in general and to theology in particular. *Thirdly* there comes a new way of experiencing theological reality that leads us to exegetical suspicion, that is, to the suspicion that the prevailing interpretation of the Bible has not taken important pieces of data into account. *Fourthly* we have our new hermeneutic, that is, our new way of interpreting the fountainhead of our faith (i.e., Scripture) with the new elements at our disposal.

The difference arises from the fact that for Segundo (1993a: 71) the origin of liberation theology was to be found in academia with the discovery of the social functions of ideologies, that is, that the whole culture, including the understanding of the Christian faith, was working for the benefit of the ruling classes. The aim of this first liberation theology was to remake the whole of theology, deideologizing the customary interpretation of the Christian faith, "the necessary task in order to get the whole Church to carry to our people an understanding of our faith both more faithful to Jesus' gospel and more capable of contributing to the humanization of all people and social classes on our continent." A shift occurred, Segundo argues, when the context of theologizing moved from the university and the middle classes to the poor and the common people and the task of deideologizing became slighted.

To clarify his hermeneutical circle, Segundo (1976: 10-34) applies the four steps of the circle to Harvey Cox, Karl Marx, Max Weber, and James Cone. He determines that only James Cone in his black liberation theology succeeds in completing the four steps of the circle. Thus he demonstrates the key to his method: the exposure of unconscious and conscious ideologies that sacralize the status quo which clears the way for the creation of new and more effective ideologies for the liberation of society and humanity. (We will elaborate on Segundo's ideological dialectic in the third section.)

From the foregoing it becomes clear that the essence of the paradigm change in liberation theology is epistemology and methodology. In the language of Kuhn, Latin American liberation theology constitutes a new exemplar in theological worldview, perspective, study, and research. Thus, Boff (1989: 38) rightly claims that the originality and specificity of liberation theology lies in an epistemological break that resulted in a new possibility of interpreting reality, a new way of doing theology. Segundo (1976: 39-40) further contends that "the one and only thing that can maintain the liberative character of any theology is not its content but its methodology. It is the latter that guarantees the continuing bite of theology, whatever terminology may be used and however much the existing system tries to absorb it into itself."

Theology Addressed to Nonpersons

Much theology, traditional and contemporary, is addressed to the non-believer. It was, and is, therefore, apologetic, aimed at demonstrating the rationality and credibility of Christian belief, if not at the eventual conversion of the non-believer into a believing member of the Church. Today, Western theology especially has to start from the challenges posed by modern unbelief: science and technology have dominated many natural forces previously thought to be controlled by, and reserved to, supernatural powers; the secularization of cultures has met many meanings and aspirations considered to be fulfilled ultimately by the transcendent; a world come of age has announced the death of God as the grave of all religion and religious institutions. What these challenges in the least demand is the purification of religious language and belief, the renewal of religious practice and life, the reform of religious structures and institutions.

Liberation theology diverges from this focus and thrust. As Gutierrez (1994: 550) has pointed out several times, quoting his most recent formulation:

> But in Latin America the challenge does not come first and foremost from nonbelievers but from "nonpersons" — that is, those whom the prevailing social order does not acknowledge as persons: the poor, the exploited, those systematically and lawfully stripped of their

human status, whose who hardly know what a human being is. Nonpersons represent a challenge, not primarily to our religious world but to our economic, social, political, and cultural world. Their existence is a call to a revolutionary transformation of the very foundations of our dehumanizing society.

In this context, then, the question is not, How are we to talk of God in a world come of age? but, How are we to proclaim God as Father (or Mother) in a nonhuman world? What is implied when we tell nonpersons that they are sons and daughters of God?

Nonpersons, the poor, the marginalized of society are, therefore, the specific interlocutors of liberation theology. It is their situation of poverty and underdevelopment that is scientifically analyzed; it is the praxis of their liberation that is critically reflected on. And Latin America and the Third World generally are today marked by "the irruption of the poor" which constitutes a special challenge to theology (Fabella and Torres 1983): the poor who until now were absent from history are making themselves present and their presence felt in their popular struggles for liberation and in the historical consciousness arising from those struggles.

But for theology to be able to address the non-person, it has first of all to be converted to the other, the non-person. There must be, at the outset, a radical option for the poor in their concrete situations as victims of injustice, which implies a new way of being a Christian, a new mode of being a theologian, a new form of doing theology. Gutierrez (1973: 198) has called attention to the parable of the Good Samaritan (Luke 10, 25-37), the inversion by Jesus of the question posed by the lawyer. The original question was: Who is my neighbor? But Jesus asked: Who of the three proved neighbor to the man who fell among the robbers? It is easy enough to love humanity in general, to love the neighbor as an abstraction. But what is demanded is to love people in the concrete, to be converted to the world of the poor.

Such a commitment has come to be known as "the preferential option for the poor," reaffirmed and enshrined as a theological, moral, and spiritual principle by the Latin American bishops at their 1979 conference at Puebla, who devoted one chapter of their final document to it (Eagleson and Scharper 1979). It has been accepted by and incorporated into the official body of the social teachings of the Catholic Church, and it has been used as an organizing principle by the U.S. Bishops in their pastoral letter on the economy, *Economic Justice for All*. There are two equally crucial aspects to the preferential option for the poor: an experiential aspect which also includes a hermeneutic aspect, and an activist or political aspect that involves action.

Regarding the first aspect which can be summed up in the word, "solidarity," Dorr (1994: 757) writes:

At the heart of the experiential aspect lies a deliberate choice to enter in some degree into the world of those who are deprived — to share in a significant way in their experience of being mistreated, bypassed, or left helpless. It springs from compassion and involves a choice to deepen this compassion by sharing to some extent in the suffering of the poor. By entering the world of deprived people one begins to experience not only their pain and struggle but also their hopes and their joys.

Experiencing the situation of the poor results in a new way of seeing social reality, that from the perspective of the poor. This is what Baum (1989; see also Baum 1987) calls the hermeneutic dimension of the preferential option for the poor, which is also a sociological principle, the basic insight of the sociology of knowledge. Knowledge is not neutral, nor completely objective, nor totally value-free. Knowledge is very often colored, oftentimes unconsciously, by one's vested interests and social position. The preferential option for the poor calls for a reading of society from below, from the underside of history, from how economic, social, and political structures marginalize, exploit, and oppress non-persons. Such a perspective yields new insights and new under-standings; in fact, a new vision of reality, if not actually a new reality, is revealed. Gutierrez (1993: 90) points this out in the life of Bartolome de las Casas, the great sixteenth-century defender of the Indians in the New World:

> Adopting the perspective of the natives of the Indies was one of the great efforts of Bartolome's life, and the principal source of his pastoral and theological creativity. Therefore when he makes the viewpoint of the "Indian oppressed" his own, his reflections acquire a new, liberated tone, and he is able to see in the message of the gospel what was otherwise hidden from him and many of his contemporaries.

The preferential option for the poor also involves and demands a commitment to take action to overcome poverty and underdevelopment, to fight injustice and oppression, to reform social structures of injustice and sin, to bring about the emancipation and liberation of the poor. Dorr (1994: 758) mentions four specific steps needed to realize the activist or political dimension of this commitment. First, there is the need for a careful analysis of the basic sources of injustice. Second, there is the need to avoid collusion with the forces responsible for the injustice. Third, there is the need for carefully planned and concerted action to challenge the injustice. Fourth, there is the need to design realistic alternatives to the unjust structures.

Solidarity with the poor, participation in their struggles is a privileged hermeneutical perspective for liberation theology, a veritable *locus theologicus*. The poor are blessed not because they are better than anybody else, nor because they possess special qualities or characteristics. The poor are blessed because of the justice of God who is not neutral in the face of oppression, and because of the reign of God which was defined in relation to the disinherited of the world. Even Segundo (1993b: 119-120), for whom the task of deideologizing is primary in the construction of liberation theology, posits that the option for the poor is the hermeneutic key for understanding the Gospel. He makes the shocking assertion that "in Latin America, literally millions of people are dying because for five centuries the gospel has been interpreted in a particular way." The option for the poor is the hermeneutic key in deideologization, "the antecedent element required in order to interpret the gospel and keep its letter from killing."

Liberation theology does not idealize the poor, nor does the preferential option for the poor romanticize poverty. The poor can be as sinful as anybody else, and they are in need of redemption as everybody else. Material poverty, like the grinding poverty that the majority of the peoples of the Third World is mired in, is a situation of degradation and dehumanization that cries out to the consciences of contemporary men and women. Gutierrez (1973: 291-302) points out that in the bible poverty is a scandalous situation that is inimical to human dignity and therefore contrary to the will of God. What is good is the opportunity it provides for spiritual childhood, "the ability to welcome God, an openness to God, a willingness to be used by God, a humility before God."

Liberation theology's option for the poor means protest against poverty and solidarity with the poor. It takes the form of protesting the degradation and dehumanization that poverty causes and inflicts. It is actualized in "being with" the poor as they struggle to correct the root causes of their situation, to lift themselves up to a level worthy of human beings, to take charge of their future and destiny. In confronting the challenges posed by non-persons, liberation theology situates them in their socio-political context. As Gutierrez (1975: 32) makes clear:

> The "poor person" is not the result of an act of fate. One's existence is not politically neutral or ethically innocent. The poor person is the product of the system in which we live and for which we are responsible. He is on the margin of our social and cultural world. Even more, the poor person is the oppressed, the exploited, the proletarian, the one deprived of the fruit of his labor and despoiled of being a person. For that reason, the poverty of the poor person is not a call for a generous act that will alleviate his suffering, but rather a demand for building a different social order.

Such an option requires a rupture from our middle-class way of living and thinking, our middle-class values and prejudices, our middle-class aspirations and tastes, our lifestyles of belongings and possessions. The break, in turn, constitutes an opening up to another world of values, another scale of priorities, another way of living and loving, of suffering and dying. But for such an option to result in a liberating praxis of love, a spirituality of risk, tension, and conflict is needed, a spirituality no longer of the individualistic, intimist, and narcissistic kind, but one that is nourished and, in turn, nourishes the socio-political processes in which one lives and through which liberation is achieved. It is no wonder, therefore, that it is in the area of liberation spirituality that there has been the most development in liberation theology (e.g. to cite only Gutierrez 1984, 1987, 1991).

To be involved with the poor in their liberation struggles does not only bring upon oneself the ire of the established socio-political order, but oftentimes also the disapproval of the equally established Church. Gutierrez (1975: 38-39) has recognized this dilemma in the lives of many Christians involved in liberation.

> There are Christians, who, while absorbed by the political demands of a liberating commitment, experience the tension produced by their solidarity with the exploited and their affiliation with the Church in which many members are linked to the established order. They lose the dynamic of their faith and suffer in anguish a dichotomy between their being Christian and acting politically. Even more cruel is the situation of those who see their love of God disappear, while their love for man which motivates them is a love which God himself originates and nourishes.

The liberation struggle is no comfortable bed nor triumphal road, and only a spirituality rooted in the love crucified on the cross can fulfill, instead of impoverish, the life and struggle for liberation. Gutierrez (1983: 225) rightly concludes that "our method is our spirituality." Such a spirituality of liberation needs to be sustained and replenished in community. Christian liberation has its roots in the communion of hearts and minds, the community of vision and aspirations, the union of efforts and resources of Christians who have made their faith the common-ground for their involvement and commitment. Thus, the emphasis on "base communities" who together hear the Word of God, celebrate the Eucharist, are united in prayer and mutual support in service to the oppressed in society. The critical reflection of a theology addressed to non-persons is rooted in such basic communities.

Theology of and **for** *Liberation*

Theology has become an academic discipline, mainly confined within the four walls of seminaries and universities. Before Vatican II, it was mostly geared to the intellectual formation of clergymen, thus making theology primarily the handmaid of the institutional Church. It too often was removed from confronting the real life-problems and the actual life-situations of people. In many cases, theological reflection simply meant the elaboration of what has been laid down officially. Theology, of course, has always posited as its ultimate objective the salvation of souls, but as practiced this has mostly meant individual morality and spiritual salvation. The societal nature of human emancipation in its economic, political, and cultural dimensions never occupied the center of the traditional theological task.

Liberation theology, by reflecting on the historical praxis of liberation and by addressing itself to nonpersons, posits as its prior value-orientation a preferential option for the poor, and directs itself to the final goal of liberation from oppression and sin. It is not only a theology *of* and *about* liberation, therefore; it is primarily and ultimately a theology *for* liberation. Just as traditional theological reflection was not simply for its own sake, but had an instrumental function, namely, the intellectual, moral, and spiritual edification of the Church community, similarly liberation theology puts itself at the service of the Christian community as the latter struggles and strives toward the goal of liberation from the structures of injustice and sin. In the hands of Jesus and the prophets, theology was not only a religious instrument, but also a social and political instrument which disturbed the socio-political establishment as they announced the Good News of salvation to the disenfranchised and the outcast.

For theology to become a theology *for* liberation, theology itself must be liberated. Thus Segundo (1976, 1992) devotes an entire book to *The Liberation of Theology* and, more recently, to *The Liberation of Dogma*. Theology must be liberated from the narrow exclusivism that it has been reduced to, both in terms of its practitioners and in terms of its content. Theology must become once more the reflection in faith of a believing community as it tries to respond through faith in Christ to the concrete problems of its members in their particular situations, as well as, to the wider cares and concerns of society at large, of peoples in the world, and of planet earth as a whole.

Here lay participation is highlighted, and the communal and ecumenical dimensions are emphasized. The laity are part and parcel of the People of God, and they have not only a duty but a right to contribute to the building up of the Body of Christ. And in an age when problems overshadow divisions and conflicts between ecclesial bodies and religions, people of different faiths have a lot to learn from each other, and have a common stake in working together against poverty and oppression.

The second implication for a theology *for* liberation is the deideologizing of religion and theology, a task emphasized in Segundo's hermeneutic circle. Liberation theology makes us aware not only of the historical and cultural conditioning of Christian teaching and preaching, but of their ideological functioning in the actual understanding and lives of people. For one thing, traditional biblical events and symbols, emptied of their socio-political content, acted as barriers for Christians to confront the social and political evils in their midst. By evading them as not central to the concerns of the Christian message, Christians effectively contributed to the human and social costs suffered by countless numbers in the course of history. The privatization and spiritualization of the Gospel, wittingly or unwittingly, void the public character of Christ's life and ministry, and in their practical consequences serve to legitimate and justify the established order, its injustices and inequalities included.

More seriously, as Gutierrez (1993: 126-153) has pointed out, with the establishment of Christianity as the state religion by the Edict of Thessalonica in 381, the Christian religion and Christian theology slowly changed focus to assume the perspective of power. Thus, the colonial wars of Spain and Portugal and the servitude of the natives of the Indies were justified as instruments in the service of the task of evangelization. From the time of the conquest, the Catholic Church in Latin America has allied itself with wealth and power, even with the terror of the National Security State, an alliance that was officially ruptured by Medellin in 1968 but which is being mended by a conservative papacy and episcopacy. In this light, Segundo's (1993b) assertion about the death of millions due to a particular interpretation of the Gospel loses its shock. In opposition to the perspective of power, he poses the option for the poor as the hermeneutic key in ideologizing and correctly interpreting the Gospel.

Toward this end, liberation theology asks how religion actually functions and operates in the lives of nonpersons, in their lives of dehumanizing poverty. Because the bible was tamed and selectively preached to them, religion generally contributes to and reinforces their passivity and resignation in the face of abuses and injustices, their patience and fatalism in their conditions of poverty and misery, their inferiority and subservience to dominant groups of wealth and power. In the religious lives of many nonpersons, liberation theology sees validity in Marx's (1963: 41) statement: "Religious suffering is at the same time an expression of religious suffering and a protest against real suffering. Religion is the sigh of the oppressed creature, the sentiment of a heartless world, and the soul of soulless conditions. It is the opium of the people."

But while the opium-aspect of religion is usually well known, liberation theology also attends to the protest-aspect of religion. It recognizes that popular religions have aspects of protest against present conditions of misery and suffering, as well as, dimensions of prophecy of a new and better world of dignity and freedom, of equality and prosperity. Popular religiosity contains seeds of liberation that can grow, flower, and bloom in liberation consciousness and liberation efforts. A theology of liberation deideologizes religion by extirpating its ideological elements and retrieving its liberative elements and incorporating them into the dignity and freedom that are at the heart of Christ's message.

Thus popular religion, specifically folk Catholicism, is not simply dismissed as outright superstition which the official Church was wont to do, nor uncritically accepted *in toto* which according to Segundo (1993a: 72-75) is the danger when the context of theologizing shifts to the common people. He warns that with the shift in the task of liberation theology that occurred with the rise of popular movements, especially of Peronism in Argentina, theologians, wanting to be the "organic intellectuals" of the poor, understand their function as simply grounding, articulating, and defending the beliefs and practices coming from popular religiosity. In the best tradition of Freire's (1971, 1973) "conscientization" and for the construction of a theology *for* liberation, the hermeneutical aspect of the preferential option for the poor also involves critiquing the religious meanings, images, and aspirations of the poor, and evaluating their directions, implications, and consequences in the light of liberation from the structures of injustice and sin.

This is true for the tools of social analysis as well, the first step in the theology of liberation. The structural-functional theory of modernization which was then dominant in development studies was rejected because it was considered ideological. Not only was it ethnocentric in that its model and its goal were the modern Western nation-state, its concepts and the understanding of the social processes involved in modernization were based on the experience of the West, but it was biased toward the stability, maintenance, and perpetuation of the status quo of power relations between nations. The conflict theory of dependency in development studies was preferred because not only did it resonate better with the experience of underdeveloped nations and peoples being a view from the underside of history, but it pointed toward the necessity of social changes for the development of Third World peoples. Thus, "ideological suspicion" permeates the perspective of a theology *for* liberation, suspicion of the ideological functioning of dominant forms of knowledge and understanding, of the entire culture, and of theology and religion.

A third implication of a theology *for* liberation concerns the relationship between faith and ideologies, the most controversial aspect of what Hennelly (1989: 41; see also Hennelly 1977a, 1977b) calls the "ideological dialectic" of Segundo. Up to now, ideology has been understood negatively and pejoratively as a system of ideas that rationalizes, justifies, and legitimates the status quo, the social structures of inequality, an understanding derived from Marx. Ideology, however, has also a positive meaning, understood as a concrete program of action directed toward social change, toward changing the status quo and the social structures of injustice and inequality. Segundo (1976: 106-122) argues that faith is dead faith without ideologies, that faith must operate in terms of ideologies. In other words, a preferential option for the poor and a theology *for* liberation must take shape and be given form in concrete programs of action.

Similarly, a theology of liberation includes the formulation of concrete socio-political programs and strategies for Assman (1976: 111-112):

> If theological reflection is to be historically and practically valid, then it has to operate on these three levels, which are 1. *the level of social, economic and political analysis* . . . 2. *The level of opting for particular theories and approaches* . . . 3. *The level of strategy and tactics* . . .

Theology cannot remain on the level of general principles. A theology *for* liberation cannot rest content with talk without action, otherwise talk becomes moralistic pieties and platitudes. Just as individual spirituality and personal morality prescribe concrete steps in growing towards spiritual maturity and in acquiring moral virtues, so social liberation needs concrete programs and strategies for its realization. Since faith must be translated into practice, since faith can only be incarnated in the lives of people with others in society, a faith-commitment to liberation must take historical forms in concrete and particular programs and strategies of and for liberation.

An abstract, universal theology based on the permanent human condition subject to pain and suffering, sin, and death is found insufficient. A particular, localized theology is meaningful and relevant to the extent that it clarifies the faith-response of people in their concrete historical conditions, insofar as it contributes to the transformation of their lives in their cultural milieu. The total and definitive liberation of humanity in Christ must be given spatial and temporal forms, and can only be mediated in concrete historical and cultural realizations. But instead of being relativized and rendered of secondary importance, the concrete realizations and historical mediations are related to, and tied up with, the absolute eschatological future in Christ. That is why there cannot be one theology of liberation, but a plurality of liberation theologies. Latin American liberation theology cannot simply be imported and transplanted as one more consumer item, although it can serve as an exemplar. In the same manner that human and social problems on earth do not admit of total, complete, and final solutions, theological clarifications, liberation theologies, and ideological programs must be content to be tentative, partial, and provisional. In place of defeatism and cooptation, this precisely constitutes the ongoing life and challenge of the theological enterprise as with all human endeavors.[2]

To put it differently: it is not only a matter of relating and tying up the need and struggle for liberation from oppression to the core of the Christian message. Nor is it only a question of revealing the social and political implications at the heart of the Gospel message in relation to the oppressive situation and the liberating practice. The re-interpreted meanings of the biblical symbols, the re-defined applications of the Christian message which result from the second step of theological reflection can only be verified in the actual practice of, and participation in, the liberation process. Theological discourse is justified and validated by social practice: since faith and life cannot be dichotomized, theology is true insofar as it makes for the faith-commitment for liberation from oppression, as it effectively contributes to the promotion of justice and the transformation of society. Historical praxis is not only the *locus theologicus* of critical reflection; it is the *locus verificationis* for theological discourse as well.

Thus a theology of liberation involves a completed hermeneutic circle and becomes a theology *for* liberation. Traditional theology unconsciously adopted partial perspectives and unwittingly served ideological functions of legitimation. Liberation theology makes conscious and explicit its own ideological orientation for liberation in concrete programs of action. As the Boffs (1984: 32) put it: "Liberation in Jesus Christ is not identified *with* political, economic, and social liberation, but it is historically identified *in* political, economic, and social liberation." Its hermeneutic thrust is to critically reflect on the present, to critically reclaim the past, and to critically create for the future.

This, however, is the most serious charge leveled at liberation theology, namely, that it instrumentalizes theology, that it reduces faith to ideology, that it is guilty of political reductionism. Theology, it is said, can never baptize any social, economic, or political system. Faith, it is added, must always maintain what is called "an eschatological reserve." Miguez Bonino (1975: 86) admits that "the 'ideologization' of the gospel is the charge most frequently brought against this theology." Hennelly (1977a) considers this to be one of the special challenges of Segundo's theology to Western theology. Similar to the charge of Marxism, this accusation is also overly simplistic and misplaced, although without proper distinctions and qualifications the danger is present.

An innovative way out of the impasse is provided by the U.S. Bishops in *The Challenge of Peace: God's Promise and Our Response* (1983) and *Economic Justice for All* (1986), their pastoral letters on nuclear arms and on the economy respectively (O'Brien and Shannon 1992). Besides their novel approach of extensive consultations in the drafting of the letters, another novelty is the distinction the bishops introduce between general principles to which it is presumed all can and will assent and policy guidelines to which they expect some disagreement and on which people in good faith can disagree. To prevent their teaching from being evacuated of any relevance and urgency, the bishops consider it important to venture into specific proposals to show how the principles are valid and are embodied.

A similar movement toward specific systems is apparent in the social teachings of the Catholic Church. The social encyclicals have been silent on, if not wary of, the political system of democracy while the Church had identified itself with regimes that were anything but democratic. And their attitude toward the economic systems of capitalism and socialism while searching for a mythical "third way" had been: "a pox on both of your houses." *Centesimus Annus* (1991), however, contains a forthright endorsement of democracy and a positive evaluation of capitalism, not in its liberal and state guises but in its social version, or what John Paul II calls "a business economy, market economy or simply free economy." It is not state capitalism characterized by the partnership of state and big business for mercantilist purposes, not is it liberal or laissez-faire capitalism where a minimal state allows the market to reign supreme, but social capitalism where the principles of subsidiarity and solidarity are operative (O'Brien and Shannon 1992: 471). The principle of subsidiarity calls for the operations of the market in the economy, whereas the principle of solidarity justifies government intervention for the common good and public policies for the disadvantaged. Thus, both pastoral letters and social encyclicals can be said, in the terminology of liberation theology, to have come full cycle in the hermeneutic circle and to have embodied their theological reflections in specific systems and concrete proposals for action.[3]

Chapter IV

ಬಂಡ

The Community Structure of the Liberation Paradigm

A paradigm is defined in terms of a community of scholars utilizing a common theoretical and procedural framework. Conversely, a community of scientists is defined in terms of the paradigm common to such a group of practitioners. Thus, the community structure of a paradigm is equal in importance to, if not more important than, the cognitive nature of the paradigm. A community of scholars makes possible the emergence and acceptance of a new paradigm amid the crisis of the old paradigm, its diffusion throughout the wider scientific community, its defense and maintenance against criticisms and opposition, and the full-blown development of its implications and consequences. This is true of the community structure of the paradigm of Latin American liberation theology.

Smith (1991) studied the emergence and survival of liberation theology as a social movement by employing the political process model of social movements in which three variables — political opportunities, insurgent consciousness, and organizational strength — are crucial in producing and sustaining a social movement. He followed liberation theology from the broad social and cultural changes in the 1950s that laid the conditions for its emergence, to its heyday in the late 1960s and early 1970s, to the time of the greatest opposition to it in the 1970s, and to the period of renewed conservatism in the Catholic Church in the 1980s that is constricting it. His discussion of the organizational strength of the movement especially elucidates the community structure of the liberation paradigm.

Many theologians who would constitute the community of scholars sharing the paradigm of liberation theology were involved in and became radicalized through Catholic Action in the 1950s and 1960s. Catholic Action was the organizational response of the Catholic Church to the social and cultural changes sweeping throughout Latin America during this period. With the establishment of national conferences of bishops and especially the continent-wide Latin American Episcopal Conference (CELAM) in 1955, they became theological advisers to bishops and staff members of the conferences. This cohort of bright, young Latin American priests went to Europe for graduate education, watched their European theological mentors radically transform the self-understanding and mission of the Catholic Church during Vatican II, and would constitute "the real leaders of the liberation theology movement" (Smith 1991: 104), although they will form a self-conscious leadership group only in the later 1960s and early 1970s. Put differently by Dussel (1992a: 155), liberation theology would become "the reflection of a whole generation of Latin American theologians, the origin of which should not be attributed to individuals." Or, liberation theology was "the theology of an ecclesial experience (especially so since 1968) on a continent-wide scale, unlike theological schools with a particular founder" (Dussel 1992b: 394).

The heyday of liberation theology was the period 1968-1972, and during this period the organized leadership of the theological movement was formed. According to Smith (1991: 168-169), out of the April 1972 meeting of Christians for Socialism in Santiago, Chile, "a single network of radical theological elites emerged with a core group that was working to elaborate and propagate the theology of liberation." A clear set of characteristics marked this first generation of about thirty-two theologians.

> First, the key members of this group were similar in age. Two consequences of this age distribution were significant. First, membership in one age cohort helped facilitate similar life experiences for these theologians, increasing the likelihood of in-group cohesion. Second, the specific age of these theologians placed them, at the right time in history, at the 'prime' of their professional lives: at Medellin they were all in their late 30s and early 40s — old enough to be experienced and respected and young enough to be highly energetic and aggressive.

In addition, according to Cleary (1985: 16-17) and my own research, almost all of these leaders were:

1. Internationally educated, usually in Europe or the United States;
2. Ordained priests, ministers, or bishops;
3. Associated with some historic public event, such as Vatican II, Medellin, or the publishing of a controversial book;
4. Ecumenically — rather than confessionally — oriented;
5. Cosmopolitan, deeply involved in the urban world;
6. Involved in international activities and organizations;
7. Sociologically-oriented;
8. Engaged in many institutional roles, such as pastor, teacher, writer, organizer, research, at the same time;
9. Members of or consultants to high-level church committees, such as institutes of CELAM, commissions carrying on the work of Vatican II, key departments of the World and National Council of Churches (Geneva and New York), or the Confederation of Evangelical Churches in Latin America;
10. Driven by a concern with the poor and oppressed (Smith 1991: 169-170).

This nucleus of leaders would articulate the vision of liberation theology, deepen its reflections, expand its concerns, legitimate its methodology, and plot out its future. They were interrelated by their ties to groups and organizations that proliferated during this period. They published a spate of periodicals, articles, and books, and organized and held conferences which facilitated its diffusion and development. They established a number of research and training institutes, and even founded publishing companies specifically devoted to liberation theology. Major international conferences were held, international communication and resource ties were set up so that liberation theology with its own localized versions became a worldwide theological phenomenon.

During this period, CELAM became, in the words of Smith (1991: 108) "*the* institutional facilitator" of liberation theology. Smith (1991: 167-168) adds that "perhaps no other Church organization worked as aggressively as CELAM to implement the vision of Medellin, and probably no other official Church organization was as insistent on clearly defining the vision of Medellin as liberationist." Sub-departments were expanded and new institutes were created, and their membership was filled by a cadre of progressive bishops and their staffs. For four years, the resources and authority of CELAM were used to promote liberation theology.

And "the prime institutional channel for popular participation" was the *base ecclesial communities* (Smith 1991: 19) which by the late 1970s had grown to between 150,000 to 200,00, with approximately 90,000 in Brazil alone. A radical innovation in ecclesiology, these basic Christian communities emphasized participation, equality, bible study, lay leadership, consciousness raising, and sociopolitical activism. They offered an excellent social and ecclesial structure for the introduction, propagation, facilitation, and survival of liberation theology (see, e.g., Torres and Eagleson 1981; Azevedo 1987).

1972 to 1979 was the time of the greatest opposition to liberation theology. The opposition came from within the Catholic Church and from without, from national security states that had been installed across Latin

America. Liberation theology was ousted from CELAM. Repression, torture, and murder became common. Priests, nuns, pastoral workers, and lay people involved in social action were assassinated. Archbishop Oscar Romero was gunned down in 1980. The repression, however, did not deal a death blow to liberation theology, but had unexpected positive effects. Brutal military actions blocked the efforts of conservative bishops to reverse the direction of Medellin and strengthened the resolve and commitment of progressive bishops. In most cases, the Catholic Church offered the only institutional protection against the blatant violation of human rights. The repression from within the Church and from military governments made liberation theologians more able to identify with the poor and strengthened the fraternal bond among them. A new generation of liberation theologians helped continue the work of reformulating the Christian message in the light of Latin America's poverty and oppression (Smith 1991: 201). The base ecclesial communities continued their quiet, steady growth. Most importantly, liberation theology saw this period of "captivity" as a spiritual passage from death to liberation; it held to the theological aphorism that "the blood of martyrs is the seed of the Church."

Liberation theology and the Latin American Church faced, and will face, new changes and new challenges in the 1980s and beyond (Steward-Gambino 1992). On the national level, there is the challenge of democratization and of the Pentecostal movement. Military regimes have given way to tenuous democratic regimes, saddled as they are with the burden of foreign debts and confronted by the more daunting task of improving the lives of their peoples. Evangelical and Pentecostal religions have made tremendous inroads into the Latin American masses and have loosened the religious monopoly of the Catholic Church. On the international level, there is a renewed conservatism with John Paul II appointing more conservative bishops and the Vatican's Congregation of the Faith actively criticizing aspects of liberation theology. As it faces these new changes and challenges, the community of Latin American liberation theologians can take heart that liberation has become a mainstream theological principle, part and parcel of normal theological science. As expressed in the conviction of Schillebeeckx (1973: 55): "In contemporary society, it is impossible to believe in Christianity which is not at one with the movement to emancipate mankind."

Conclusion

ഇൗൽ

T his monograph sought to explain Latin American liberation theology, the most significant innovation in contemporary theology, by utilizing Kuhn's theory of scientific revolutions, but also by going beyond it to include the wider social and institutional context of theology. As an exercise in Kuhnian sociology of science, the monograph discussed both the cognitive nature and the community structure of the paradigm of liberation theology. At the heart of the paradigm change in Latin American liberation theology is method, a new way of doing theology. Thus, the paradigm of liberation theology is primarily exemplar, the central element in Kuhn's understanding of paradigm.

The analogous application of the theory of paradigm change further clarifies a number of points. First, a new paradigm arouses opposition from the old paradigm; it creates polarization among the practitioners of normal science (Kuhn 1970: 93). A new paradigm overthrows traditional assumptions, symbols, values, and methods. A new paradigm also overturns the established definition of science and the self-conception of scientists. A new paradigm radically changes the perception of the nature of the reality being studied. Thus, paradigm change can account for the fierce denunciation, even deadly opposition, to Latin American liberation theology. Geffre (1974: 16) noted that Western theology was well tempted to disregard it as an "anti-theology."

Second, paradigms in the natural sciences are incommensurable; a victorious new paradigm completely displaces the old exhausted paradigm (Kuhn 1970: 150). In the social sciences, however, there is a multiplicity of paradigms because of the different nature of the subject matter, i.e. human behavior, under study. Besides, paradigms, as concrete examples of scholarship, are not discipline-wide, but sub-disciplinary (Eckberg and Hill 1980: 130). Similarly, liberation theology has not displaced the older theological paradigms, but has taken its place among the paradigms of normal theological science, with its implications impacting them (Fiorenza 1991).

Third, a paradigm is constitutive of science (Kuhn 1970: 110). A paradigm is not a mere neutral, passive, disembodied analytical tool. A paradigm, in specifying metatheoretical presuppositions, shared commitments, and concrete examples, constitutes the science, determines the scientific task, and defines the scientist. Paradigm change, in other words, involves a rupture in scientific conceptual webs. At the heart, therefore, of the scientific revolutionary process is a demand for a radical conversion of scientific outlook. Thus, the paradigm of liberation theology implies, indeed demands, a new way of looking at theology, a new way of doing theology, and a new way of being a theologian.

Fourth, a paradigm is constitutive of nature (Kuhn 1970: 110). A paradigm is our way of looking at nature or reality. It determines therefore what we see, and defines the reality that we see. The reality that is the subject of study is constituted by the paradigm that is used. Paradigm change, in other words, involves a change in *weltanschauung*; it demands a conversion, a gestalt switch in worldviews. In the same manner, the paradigm of liberation theology opens up realities hitherto hidden from theological view, retrieves theological truths obscured by the older theological paradigms, and sees vistas of theological reality unimagined by extant theological vision. Herein perhaps lies the greatest contribution of Latin American liberation theology, the blazing of new theological trails, assiduously being pursued by other liberation theologies.[4]

Notes

1   This needs to be clarified. Cone published *Black Theology and Black Power* in 1969, and *A Black Theology of Liberation* in 1970. It remains true, however, that Latin American liberation theology popularized and legitimated the idea and method of liberation theology.

2   In this connection, it is important to point out that Paul VI in *Octogesima Adveniens* (1971) located responsibility for the analysis and solution of social problems in local communities and churches: "It is up to the Christian communities to analyze with objectivity the situation which is proper to their own country, to shed on it the light of the Gospel's unalterable words and to draw principles of reflection, norms of judgment and directions for action from the social teaching of the Church" (O'Brien and Shannon 1992: 266).

Elsbernd (1995: 39) notes, however, that this "central expression of a historically conscious methodology in magisterial teaching" is undergoing intentional distortion and reversal under John Paul II. She ends by saying that "the credibility and integrity of Catholic social teaching requires that it retrieve the fundamental insights sketched in *Gaudium et Spes* and elaborated in *Octogesima Adveniens*" (Elsbernd 1995: 60).

3   Latin American liberation theologians do not necessarily agree with this. The Boff brothers, Clodovis and Leonardo, for example, have criticized the U.S. bishops' pastoral letter on the economy for its lack of a structural analysis of American political economy. By not undertaking an analysis and critical understanding of what capitalism really represents, the letter does not call the system into question, but simply rehabilitates it (see Berryman 1989: 124; McCarthy and Rhodes 1992: 106-107). Socialism was, and is, held to embody better the utopian ideals of a liberated society. But with the collapse of the Soviet Union, with the absence of any really existing socialist society in the world today, liberation theology has

to realize that there are different kinds of capitalism, different ways of organizing a market economy, and that democracy offers space for a civil society of participation (see Hollenbach 1992). In Latin America, capitalism has been synonymous with social injustice and democracy has been an oligarchical facade for exploitation. Liberation theology has to come to grip with the full dimensions of democracy and the market, develop a better understanding and appreciation of their possibilities, and work for their liberative realizations in the concrete lives of peoples.

4   This is especially true of feminist theology which is opening up unchartered theological territory, and may have the most impact on theology in the long run (see, e.g., LaCugna 1993).

References

Abbott, Walter M., ed. 1966. *The Documents of Vatican II*. Association Press.

Assman, Hugo. 1976. *Theology for a Nomad Church*. Maryknoll, NY: Orbis Books.

Azevedo, Marcello deC., S.J. 1987. *Basic Ecclesial Communities in Brazil: The Challenge of a New Way of Being Church*. Washington, DC: Georgetown University Press.

Barbour, Ian. 1990. *Religion in an Age of Science*, The Gifford Lectures, Vol. I. San Francisco: HarperCollins.

Baum, Gregory. 1987. *Theology and Society*. New York: Paulist Press.

———. 1989. "Sociology and Salvation: Do We Need a Catholic Sociology?" *Theological Studies* 50:4 (December)

Berryman, Phillip. 1987. *Liberation Theology*. New York: Pantheon Books.

———. 1989. *Our Unfinished Business: The U.S. Catholic Bishops' Letters on Peace and the Economy*. New York: Pantheon Books.

Boff, Leonardo. 1989. "The Originality of the Theology of Liberation." In *The Future of Liberation Theology: Essays in Honor of Gustavo Gutierrez*, ed. Marc H. Ellis and Otto Maduro. Maryknoll, NY: Orbis Books.

Boff, Leonardo, and Clodovis Boff. 1984. *Salvation and Liberation: In Search of a Balance between Faith and Politics*. Maryknoll, NY: Orbis Books.

———. 1987. *Introducing Liberation Theology*. Maryknoll, NY: Orbis Books.

Brown, Robert McAfee. 1978. *Theology in a New Key: Responding to Liberation Themes*. Philadelphia: The Westminster Press.

———. 1990. *Gustavo Gutierrez: An Introduction to Liberation Theology*. Maryknoll, NY: Orbis Books.

Cadorette, Curt. 1988. *From the Heart of the People: The Theology of Gustavo Gutierrez*. Oak Park, IL: Meyer-Stone Books.

Cardoso, Fernando Henrique. 1973. "Associated-Dependent Development: Theoretical and Practical Implications." In *Authoritarian Brazil*, ed. Alfred Stepan. New Haven, CT: Yale University Press.

Cardoso, Fernando Henrique, and Enzo Faletto. 1979. *Dependency and Development in Latin America*. Enlarged ed. Berkeley, CA: University of California Press.

CELAM (Conferencia Episcopal Latino-Americana). 1970. *The Church in the Present-Day Transformation of Latin America in the Light of the Council*: Vol I: Position Papers; Vol. II: Conclusions. Bogota: General Secretariat of CELAM. Distributed by the Latin American Bureau of the United States Catholic Conference, Washington, DC.

Cleary, Edward L. 1985. *Crisis and Change: The Church in Latin America Today*. Maryknoll, NY: Orbis Books.

Cone, James H. 1969. *Black Theology and Black Power*. New York:The Seabury Press.

———. 1970. *A Black Theology of Liberation*. Philadelphia: J.B. Lippincott.

Dorr, Donal. 1994. "Poor, Preferential Option for." In *The New Dictionary of Catholic Social Thought*, ed. Judith A. Dwyer. Collegeville, MN: The Liturgical Press.

Dussel, Enrique. 1992a. "From the Second Vatican Council to the Present Day." In *The Church in Latin America, 1492-1992*, ed.Enrique Dussel. Maryknoll, NY: Orbis Books.

———. 1992b. "Recent Latin American Theology." In *The Church in Latin America, 1492-1992*, ed. Enrique Dussel. Maryknoll, NY: Orbis Books.

Eagleson, John, and Phillip Scharper, ed. 1979. *Puebla and Beyond: Documentation and Commentary*. Maryknoll, NY: Orbis Books.

Eckberg, Douglas Lee, and Lester Hill, Jr. 1980. "The Paradigm Concept and Sociology: A Critical Review." In *Paradigms and Revolutions: Appraisals and Applications of Thomas Kuhn's Philosophy of Science*, ed. Gary Gutting. Notre Dame, IN: University of Notre Dame Press.

Elsbernd, Mary. 1995. "Whatever happened to *Octogesima Adveniens?" Theological Studies* 56:1 (March)

Evans, Peter B. 1979. *Dependent Development: The Alliance of Multinational, State and Local Capital in Brazil*. Princeton, NJ: Princeton University Press.

———. 1993. "Dependency." In *The Oxford Companion to Politics of the World*, ed. Joel Krieger. New York: Oxford University Press.

Fabella, Virginia, and Sergio Torres, ed. 1983. *Irruption of the Third World: Challenge to Theology*. Maryknoll, NY: Orbis Books.

Fiorenza, Francis Schussler. 1991. "Systematic Theology: Task and Methods." In *Systematic Theology: Roman Catholic Perspectives*, Vol I, ed. Francis Schussler Fiorenza and John P. Galvin. Minneapolis: Fortress Press.

Freire, Paulo. 1971. *Pedagogy of the Oppressed*. New York: Herder and Herder.

———. 1973. *Education for Critical Consciousness*. London: Sheed and Ward.

Foster-Carter, Aidan. 1976. "From Rostow to Gunder Frank: Conflicting Paradigms in the Analysis of Underdevelopment," *World Development* 4:3 (March)

Frank, Andre Gunder. 1969a. *Capitalism and Underdevelopment in Latin America*. New York: Monthly Review Press.

———. 1969b. "The Development of Underdevelopment." In *Underdevelopment or Revolution*. New York: Monthly Review Press. First published in 1966.

Geffre, Claude. 1974. "Editorial: A Prophetic Theology." In *The Mystical and Political Dimension of the Christian Faith*, Concilium No. 96, ed. Claude Geffre and Gustavo Gutierrez. New York: Herder and Herder.

Gremillion, Joseph, ed. 1976. *The Gospel of Peace and Justice: Catholic Social Teaching Since Pope John*. Maryknoll, NY: Orbis Books.

Gutierrez, Gustavo. 1973. *A Theology of Liberation: History, Politics, and Salvation*. Maryknoll, NY: Orbis Books.

66 *References*

———. 1975. "Faith as Freedom: Solidarity with the Alienated and Confidence in the Future," *Horizons* 2:1 (Spring)

———. 1983. "Reflections from a Latin American Perspective: Finding Our Way to Talk about God." In *Irruption of the Third World: Challenge to Theology*, ed. Virginia Fabella and Sergio Torres. Maryknoll, NY: Orbis Books.

———. 1984. *We Drink from Our Own Wells: The Spiritual Journey of a People*. Maryknoll, NY: Orbis Books.

———. 1987. *On Job: God-Talk and the Suffering of the Innocent*. Maryknoll, NY: Orbis Books.

———. 1988. *A Theology of Liberation: History, Politics, and Salvation*. 15th anniversary edition with a new introduction. Maryknoll, NY: Orbis Books.

———. 1990. "Theology and the Social Sciences." In *The Truth Shall Make You Free: Confrontations*. Maryknoll, NY: Orbis Books. First published in 1984.

———. 1991. *The God of Life*. Maryknoll, NY: Orbis Books.

———. 1993. *Las Casas: In Search of the Poor of Jesus Christ*. Maryknoll, NY: Orbis Books.

———. 1994. "Liberation Theology." In *The New Dictionary of Catholic Social Thought*, ed. Judith A. Dwyer. Collegeville, MN: The Liturgical Press.

Gutting, Gary, ed. 1980. *Paradigms and Revolutions: Appraisals and Applications of Thomas Kuhn's Philosophy of Science*. Notre Dame, IN: University of Notre Dame Press.

Hennelly, Alfred T. 1977a. "The Challenge of Juan Luis Segundo," *Theological Studies* 38:1 (March)

———. 1977b. "Theological Method: The Southern Exposure," *Theological Studies* 38:4 (December)

———. 1989. *Theology for a Liberating Church: The New Praxis of Freedom*. Washington, DC: Georgetown University Press.

———, ed. 1990. *Liberation Theology: A Documentary History*. Maryknoll, NY: Orbis Books.

———, ed. 1993. *Santo Domingo and Beyond: Documents and Commentaries*. Maryknoll, NY: Orbis Books.

Hollenbach, David, S.J. 1992. "Christian Social Ethics after the Cold War," *Theological Studies* 53:1 (March)

King, M.D. 1980. "Reason, Tradition, and the Progressiveness of Science." In *Paradigms and Revolutions: Appraisals and Applications of Thomas Kuhn's Philosophy of Science*, ed. Gary Gutting. Notre Dame, IN: University of Notre Dame Press.

Kuhn, Thomas S. 1970. *The Structure of Scientific Revolutions*, 2nd edition, enlarged. Chicago: The University of Chicago Press. First published in 1962.

Kung, Hans, and David Tracy. 1989. *Paradigm Change in Theology: A Symposium for the Future*. New York: Crossroad.

Kung, Hans. 1992. *Judaism: Between Yesterday and Tomorrow*. New York: Crossroad.

———. 1995. *Christianity: Essence, History and Future*. New York: Crossroad.

LaCugna, Catherine Mowry, ed. 1993. *Freeing Theology: The Essentials of Theology in Feminist Perspective*. San Francisco: HarperCollins.

Lernoux, Penny. 1980. *Cry of the People*. New York: Doubleday.

Marx, Karl. 1963. *Selected Writings in Sociology and Social Philosophy*, ed. T. B. Bottomore and Maximilien Rudel. Middlesex, England: Penguin Books.

Masterman, Margaret. 1970. "The Nature of a Paradigm." In *Criticism and the Growth of Knowledge*, ed. Imre Lakatos and Alan Musgrave. Cambridge: Cambridge University Press.

McCarthy, George E., and Royal W. Rhodes. 1992. *Eclipse of Justice: Ethics, Economics, and the Lost Traditions of American Catholicism*. Maryknoll, NY: Orbis Books.

McGovern, Arthur F. 1989a. "Dependency Theory, Marxist Analysis, and Liberation Theology." In *The Future of Liberation Theology: Essays in Honor of Gustavo Gutierrez*, ed. Marc H. Ellis and Otto Maduro. Maryknoll, NY: Orbis Books.

———. 1989b. *Liberation Theology and Its Critics: Toward an Assessment*. Maryknoll, NY: Orbis Books.

Merton, Robert K. 1973. *The Sociology of Science: Theoretical and Empirical Investigations*. Chicago: The University of Chicago Press.

————. 1985. *On the Shoulders of Giants: A Shandean Postscript.* New York: Hartcourt Brace Jovanovich. First published in 1965.

Miguez Bonino, Jose. 1975. *Doing Theology in a Revolutionary Situation.* Philadelphia: Fortress Press.

O'Brien, David J., and Thomas A. Shannon, ed. 1992. *Catholic Social Thought: The Documentary Heritage.* Maryknoll, NY: Orbis Books.

Packenham, Robert A. 1992. *The Dependency Movement: Scholarship and Politics in Development Studies.* Cambridge, MA: Harvard University Press.

Schillebeeckx, Edward. 1973. "Critical Theories and Christian Political Commitment." In *Political Commitment and Christian Community*, Concilum No. 84, ed. Alois Muller and Norbert Greinacher. New York: Herder and Herder.

Segundo, Juan Luis. 1974. "Capitalism-Socialism: A Theological Crux." In *The Mystical and Political Dimension of the Christian Faith*, Concilum No. 96, ed. Claude Geffre and Gustavo Gutierrez. New York: Herder and Herder.

————. 1976. *The Liberation of Theology.* Maryknoll, NY: Orbis Books.

————. 1992. *The Liberation of Dogma.* Maryknoll, NY: Orbis Books.

————. 1993a. "The Shift within Latin American Liberation Theology." In *Signs of the Times: Theological Reflections.* Maryknoll, NY: Orbis Books. First published in 1983.

————. 1993b. "The Option for the Poor: Hermeneutical Key for Understanding the Gospel." In *Signs of the Times: Theological Reflections.* Maryknoll, NY: Orbis Books. First published in 1986.

Smith, Christian. 1991. *The Emergence of Liberation Theology: Radical Religion and Social Movement Theory.* Chicago: The University of Chicago Press.

Steeman, Theodore. 1973. "Political Relevance of the Christian Community between Integralism and Critical Commitment." In *Political Commitment and Christian Community*, Concilium No. 84, ed. Alois Muller and Norbert Greinacher. New York: Herder & Herder.

Stewart-Gambino, Hannah. 1992. "Introduction: New Game, New Rules." In *Conflict and Competition: The Latin American Church in a Changing Environment*, ed. Edward L. Cleary and Hannah Stewart-Gambino. Boulder, CO: Lynne Rienner Publishers.

Todaro, Michael P. 1989. *Economic Development in the Third World*. 4th ed. New York: Longman.

Torres, Sergio, and John Eagleson, ed. 1981. *The Challenge of Basic Christian Communities*. Maryknoll, NY: Orbis Books.

Tracy, David. 1975. *Blessed Rage for Order: The New Pluralism in Theology*. New York: The Seabury Press.

Weingart, Peter. 1974. "On a Sociological Theory of Scientific Change." In *Social Processes of Scientific Development*, ed. R. Whitley. London: Routledge and Kagan Paul.

Index

About the Author

M. D. Litonjua holds Licentiates in Philosophy and Theology from the University of Santo Tomas (Manila), a Ph.D. in Sociology from Brown University, and an M.B.A. from the University of Missouri-St. Louis. Originally from the Philippines, he taught at the Ateneo de Manila University. He is presently Associate Professor of Sociology at the College of Mount St. Joseph in Cincinnati, Ohio, where he teaches at the Departments of Behavioral Sciences and of Religious Studies. His latest article, "Outside the Den of Dragons: The Philippines and the NICs of Asia," appeared in *Studies in Comparative International Development*.